REND RENDER RENDER
RENDING RENDERED
RENDING RENDERING
RENDLES REND RENDERER
RENDEZVOUS RENDED
RENDERING RENDER REND
RENDY RENDRY RENDITION
RENDERABLE RENDIBLE
RENDED RENDEZVOUS
RENDEZVOUSING RENDEZ-
VOUSER RENDINGLY
RENDLING RENDER SET
RENDER SET RENDLEWOOD
RENDIBLE RENDROCK
RENDZINA RENDU RENDU-
OSLER-WEBER RENDANG

RENDANG

Will Harris

GRANTA

Granta Publications, 12 Addison Avenue, London W 11 4Q R

First published in Great Britain by Granta Books, 2020

A CIP catalogue record for this book is
available from the British Library.

10   9   8   7   6   5   4   3   2   1

ISBN 978 1 78378 559 9
eISBN 978 1 84708 560 5

Typeset in Minion by Patty Rennie

Printed and bound in Great Britain by T J International, Padstow

CONTENTS

In West Sumatra they call rendang
   randang. Neither shares a root

with rending. Rose and rose
   have French and Frisian roots

you can't hear. Context makes
   the difference clear. Here lies one

whose name was writ in *bahasa*.
   Here are words I've said

in memory of her who I could
   never speak to. Tjandra Sari,

I call you wrongly. Rend me
   rightly. Rootless and unclear.

1/

Holy Man

Everywhere was coming down with Christmas, the streets
and window displays ethereal after rain, but what was it –
October? Maybe I'd been thinking about why I hated
Tibetan prayer flags and whether that was similar to how
I felt about Christmas: things become meaningless severed
from the body of ritual, of belief. Then I thought about
those who see kindness in my face, or see it as unusually
calm, which must have to do with that image of the Buddha
smiling. I turned off Regent Street and onto Piccadilly,
then down a side road by Costa to Jermyn Street, where
a man caught my eye as I was about to cross the road
and asked to shake my hand. *You have a kind face*, he said.

Really. He was wearing a diamond-checked golfer's jumper
and said he was a holy man. As soon as he let go, he started
scribbling in a notepad, then tore out a sheet which
he scrunched into a little ball and pressed to his forehead
and the back of his neck before blowing on it – once, sharply –
and giving it to me. *I see kindness in you, but also bad habits.*
Am I right? Not drinking or drugs or sex, not like that, but bad
habits. 2020 will be a good year for you. Don't cut your hair
on a Tuesday or Thursday. Have courage. He took out his wallet
and showed me a photograph of a temple, in front of which
stood a family. His, I think. A crowd of businessmen
flowed around us. *Name a colour of the rainbow. Any colour,*

except red or orange. He was looking to my right, at what
I thought could be a rainbow – despite the sun, a light wind
blew the rain about like scattered sand – but when
I followed his gaze it seemed to be fixed on either a fish
restaurant or a suit display, or maybe backwards in time to
the memory of a rainbow. Why did he stop me? I'd been
dawdling, staring at people on business lunches. Restaurants
like high-end clinics, etherized on white wine. I must
have been the only one to catch his eye, to hold it. What
colour could I see? I tried to picture the full spectrum
arrayed in stained glass, shining sadly, and then refracted
through a single shade that appeared to me in the form of

a freshly mown lawn, a stack of banknotes, a cartoon
frog, a row of pines, an unripe mango, a septic wound. I saw
the glen beside the tall elm tree where the sweetbriar
smells so sweet, then the lane in Devon where my dad
grew up, and the river in Riau where my mum played.
It was blue and yellow mixed, like Howard Hodgkin's version
of a Bombay sunset, or pistachio ice cream; a jade statue
of the Buddha. I remembered being asked – forced – to give
my favourite colour by a teacher (why did it matter?),
which was the colour of my favourite Power Ranger,
of the Knight beheaded by Gawain, of the girdle given
to him by Lady Bertilak, and chose the same again.

The paper in your hand, if it is your colour, will bring you luck,
and if not . . . He trailed off. *First hold it to your forehead,*
then the back of your neck. Then blow. I unscrunched the ball.
Now put it here, he said, opening his wallet, *and money please.*
I had no cash. *Nothing?* He looked me in the eyes and said
(again) that he was a holy man. I felt honour-bound
to give him something. Up and down the street, men rode
to their important offices. I told him it was my favourite
colour, or had been, and as I did I saw us from a distance,
as we might seem years from now – scraps of coloured fabric
draped across a hall which, taken out of context, signified
nothing – and I flinched, waiting for the blade to fall.

Mother Country

The shades open for landing,
I see the pandan-leafed
interior expanding
towards the edge of a relieved
horizon. Down along
the banks of the Ciliwung
are slums I had forgotten,
the river like a loosely
sutured wound. As we begin
our descent into the black
smog of an emerging
power, I make out the tin
shacks, the stalls selling juices,
the red-tiled colonial
barracks, the new mall.
It is raining profusely.
After years of her urging
me to go, me holding back,
I have no more excuses.

State-Building

Break a vase, says Derek Walcott, *and the love*
that reassembles the fragments will be stronger than
that love which took its symmetry for granted.
When I read this, I can only think *who broke it?*

In the British Museum, two black 'figures'
(they don't say *slaves*) beat olives from a tree;
a 'naked youth' stoops to gather the fallen
fruit. The freeborn men elsewhere, safe behind

their porticos, argue about the world's
true form, or talk of bee glue, used
to seal the hive against attack, later called
propolis, meaning that it has to come
before – is crucial for – the building of a state.

*

Here it's summer and bees groan inside
the carcass of a split bin bag. A figure passes,
is close to passed, when I see her face, half
shadow, marked with sweat or tears, the folds

beneath each downcast eye the same light
brown as – oceans off – my grandma. *Mak.*
Give me a love that's unassimilated, sharp
as broken pots. That can't be taken; granted.

My dad would work among the blue and white
pieces of a Ming vase – his job to get it
passable. He'd gather every bit and after days
assembling, filling in (putty, spit, glue),
draw forth – not sweetness – something new.

Lines of Flight

Mariinsky Canal

A girl twists a stalk of rye
around her wrist like
a bracelet. She sees her father
at the plough and wants

to pick a cornflower, its dark
blue almost purple
colour threaded through
with grief, among the weeds.

She wants to go and pin
one to his chest. And all this
is implied, though
the photograph itself

shows just a field of rye
with cornflowers.

Diyarbakır

One day, a white rabbit read
my fortune, twitching as it chose

from several slips of paper, soft head
straining at its harness, nose

scabbed, peeled back like bark.
Here, amid the desert, stark

as day, they tortured dissidents;
now paper slips blow between

the points of a barbed wire fence.
A life should not just be, but mean.

Illinois

The familiar, unearthly
scent of *Bayside Breeze*.
On the freeway, bent
along its axis, I do

as ghosts do: wait.
Acres of still corn.
Slow-smelling night.
Across the ocean

he lies in hospital.
He might as well be
dead. This far from
the side of any bay,

I measure sweetness
by its incongruity.

London

A shuttle flies between
the seasons, smoothest
from spring to summer

when I think of my Chinese
forebears forced to work
a loom. Who'd be alone

today? Migratory birds are
weaving new patterns
in the air, shuttles flying

back and forth. Here. No,
there. I've been missing you.

My Name Is Dai

I heard him say his name was die, and seconds later that it was short for
David, spelt *D-A-I*. We had just sat down when he walked up to me
and Susie. He said he recognized her from the National Portrait Gallery.
The one with the large forehead above the door. People miss it. The sad
smile. Beer sloshed against the edges of his glass like a fish trying to
escape its bowl, but in this case the fish was dead and only looked to be
alive because of Dai's swaying. There are people who relieve themselves
of information like a dog pissing against a streetlamp to mark out
territory, urination no longer in the service of the body, providing no
relief. Likewise, conversation. Dai was a type of Ancient Mariner.

It was in his bones. He'd been working on a site with Polish builders
and it was one of their birthdays. He mimed plunking bottles on the table.
Vodka. Whole bottles? *I'm Welsh*, he said. *I was born on a mountain.
Between two sheepdogs*. He started talking about the village he grew up
in, how happy he was among the meadows and milking cows, how
unhappy he was at school. *You might've heard of one boy from school.
A right goody. Spoke like Audrey Hepburn or Shakespeare. We all bullied
him, but my mam would say why don't you be like Michael, why don't you
be like Michael. Michael bloody Sheen. Michael's shirts were always
clean and ironed. Anthony Hopkins, he was a local too. A tiny village,*

*and who came out of it? Those two and me. You know, I probably know
more words than anyone in this pub. Look at them. You think any of these
cunts can spell verbiage?* He spat out each letter – *V-E-R-B-I-A-G-E* –
and in the act of spelling became self-conscious. He turned to Susie.
What do you do? She was a writer so he told her more words. I said
I taught a little and wrote. *Teach me*, he said. *Go on*. But I couldn't think of
anything wise or useful to tell Dai. On the verge of tipping over, he
held a hand out towards us. *Tenderness*, he said, *try a little tenderness,*

and then repeating it, half singing it, he said it in a voice both louder and more tender. *That's my advice. You know who that is? Otis Redding.*

Try a little tenderness, mmm nuh uh uh. That was when Susie saw the haze descend. Like an explosion in a quarry the inward collapse rippled out across his face, throwing clouds of dust into the sky. *I'm sorry. A man shouldn't cry. I haven't cried since I was a boy. I haven't . . .* He stopped. *A man should be a brick, a boulder.* He made his hand into a fist like he was playing rock-paper-scissors in the schoolyard. *My ex-wife died last month. The funeral was yesterday. We were together twenty years but her family, her bloody family, wouldn't let me near it. God*, he said, *I loved that woman.* He couldn't say her name. He was swaying. I got the impression that he saw

his life as a sea voyage during which he'd done many strange, inexplicable and stupid things, of which shooting an albatross was one. But perhaps he knew it was better to have shot that albatross through the heart and be able to talk about it than to bear it having entered his life and gone. It was then I saw the TV and pointed. *Look! Michael Sheen.* It was true. There he was on *The One Show* in a freshly ironed shirt, smiling at Matt Baker. Dai turned around. *I'm sorry. I don't know what came over me. I need some air.* He stared at us. *You're writers,* he said. *You should write about this.* And though it may have been unfair, I thought about how many people he'd said this to before.

The White Jumper

Running and jumping from one grassy
    platform to another I stop. On
the next patch of grass. Branches so
    arranged as to focus a beam of light
on the grass. White and gleaming
    against the green. The white
jumper. The white jumper. The white

We were at a pizza restaurant for Hugo's birthday.

Dan said he was coming back from work. A late shift at
the hospital. Then a car came towards him at the crossing.
He stood his ground and the next thing he knows he's
shouting and the arsehole's driving off. In the ambulance
they're telling him not to look down. *Mate, look here.*
Look here, mate. Laid up for six months. It went to the High
Court. It was two years before he got compensation.

I looked across at Hugo. I looked out of the window.

Next week Dan flies to Australia. Four months. No
time to waste. He's going to finish his novel. It's about
a time-travelling wood elf. You know how relativity
works. Space folds over on itself. The US military had
this plan to nuke the moon. It all happened during
the Cold War. They didn't plan on it being overcast.

I looked across at Hugo. I looked out of the window.

We were sitting upstairs and in the whitest end-of-day light
the walls white too it felt not just like we were above
ground but that despite being in Covent
Garden we were on a ridge above a
forest looking down our feet in
thicket dark our heads
in thickest
stars

I hadn't seen Hugo in years.

At primary school, we would stay up late and play
Sonic the Hedgehog, passing the controller back and forth
when one of us died. Run, jump, jump, run, jump, run.

One night, his grandma screamed at us in Urdu.
She wore a plain white nightie.

We stopped laughing, or we tried laughing quietly.

By the time we had completed a level,
we could run through each jump without looking.

On the way home I ran past
        a Pret, a Spaghetti House,
        a Five Guys, a Bella Italia.

The path lit by the lights of passing cars,
the pith of a discarded pizza.

Pret, Spaghetti House, Five Guys, Bella Italia.

Crossing the road a car honked,
its owner shouting through his closed window

   Look where you're going, cunt.

I was looking for the white jumper.

        Phoebe recounts a dream:

        Darth Vader was chasing me through
        a tall building and I was going to take
        the lift but then he threw a knife at
        the ground-floor button, so I drew him
        up one flight of stairs and ran down
        the other, where I saw a little boy
        playing with lighter fluid, so I grabbed
        the can and dribbled it by the exit and
        set it on fire and ran outside.

Are some dreams more trivial than others?
Last night I dreamt that Morrissey was performing
and I stood behind him waving my arms in sync.
Fuck this, he said, and stormed offstage.

The Nazis admired Caspar David Friedrich for his *blood and soil* vision.

In several paintings two friends contemplate the moon, which seems to be exploding.

One shows the blast in its white heat; another has the sky a darker blue, the moon dark too.

The moon is down. I have not heard the clock. A friend rests his hand against another's shoulder to console him.

I know that *blood* stands for race and *soil* for nation but *blood and soil* makes me

think of bloodied soil. Do some people imagine themselves
in the same relation to their place of birth as a scab to a wound?

Bob recounts a dream:

I see a green meadow and a white coffin.
I am afraid that my mother is in it, but I open the lid
and luckily it is not my mother but me.

I asked my grandma questions,
my mum translating. I asked if
she was scared. *Of what?*
The coup. *No, she was brave.*
In Sumatra once, having
paid our respects at the tomb
of her husband, we drove into
the jungle. Everywhere was
green. We stopped by a store
and the driver left us to
buy water. Men walked out
from behind a pick-up truck.
She gripped the overhead
handle. Their machetes gleamed.
She gripped the overhead
handle. Everywhere was green.

In the last weeks,
bedbound, her hair
grew out, black
strands white at
the roots. Later
they lay her in
a white-frilled
coffin in a marble
room and marked
the forty days
of mourning
wearing only
white.

Lid and lip are little words. Little
things, too. The short *i* associated with
lightness and pith.

The pith of my system, said Coleridge,
is to make the senses out of the mind
– not the mind out of the senses.

The mind's white
    rind, not the white
        rind's mind.

I want to call her closed lids
buds because shut
they look like petals
tucked away which could
at any moment bud.
At her wake she asked for
pearls to be placed
inside her nostrils
and between her lips
and on her lids to light
her to the afterlife
and stop her eyes from
growing in this world again.

In April, children chased each other round the garden.

I thought of
                    the white jumper
and
                    the black hood worn by hangmen

to hide the world and keep its wearer hidden,
to denote sin and keep it out.

Théophile Gautier dreamt of white swan-women
singing and swimming down the Rhine, each one
whiter than white down but one among them

clair de lune, pure, trailing boreal fumes, breasts
like bunched camellias – a blanched battle
of satin and Paros marble, communion host

and candle. Of what white was her whiteness
made? Pallor of alabaster. Duvet of dove. Lactic
drop and lily. Crystal ondine. Mother of God.

 At the end of 2001, people gathered
 outside the mosque. A mother pushing a pram
 held a white placard in her other hand.

 I watched her from my parents' room,
 the sky like drinking water through a straw.

Karmar dragged his keyboard up the hill. I went through
my set. The poem about my ill dad, my dead gran,
my mum spilling prawn toast. Afterwards, we ate
vegetable curry and spring rolls at the Victoria Hotel
and Nabeela took us to a shisha bar on the other
side of town. Going in, she pointed to the building
opposite. Derelict. One floor lit. *It's full of junkies.*
A photographer came here last week, she said.
He'd come all the way from El Salvador to Bradford.

At night, I hear the dual carriageway beneath my window.
Torque of rubber on tarmac. Wind running through
the salt mills and dead grass. Rows of empty buildings.

To Let   To Let   For Sale

Each sign like the dedication in a second-hand book.

To   To   For

To   To   For

After the show I talked to Antony.
He was from Angola but grew up in Porto.
He worked at Carphone Warehouse.
He loved music and spent his spare time
making beats on GarageBand.

I freestyle. I never sit down and write.
How do you do it? What makes you want to write?

One time my dad held my head
   over the sink and washed
my mouth out with soap and

one time I ran and got as far as the end
   of the street and sat on
the stone steps of the mosque and

one time I dreamt about a white
   jumper on a ledge too
far away to reach and

Watching *Robot Wars*, a knock came at the door.

Opening it, hot air billowed in like orange parachute
silk. We ferried water from the kitchen. Flames
already running up the walls. Run, jump, run.

Friedrich Nietzsche recounts a dream:

Once the distance between us was so small
you could have crossed over to me
by footbridge.

Cross it, I said to you.
Cross over to me.
But you didn't want to.

And when I asked again, you were silent.

Now mountains and rivers have come
between us, and at the mention
of the footbridge you cry.

The next morning in the breakfast queue,
the man taking room numbers asked why I was
in town. I said there was a poetry reading.
That's odd, he said, and moved on to a children's
writer. At Leeds, a kid was hanging by the barriers.
The station manager jogged towards him.
I asked Karmar what he was doing. *Being a little
rascal.* The kid made to walk away before
spinning back, then jumped the barrier and ran.

Run. Jump. Run. Run. Run.

2/

Seven Dreams of Richard Spencer

1

Once I woke up with the actual gilded horns
of a cuck and you admired them and assured me
I need not fear dreams that pass through the horned
gates, but then I turned into a yellow cowfish,
flopping on the bed, and you picked me up
by my small horns and flushed me down the toilet.

2

Once I believed myself to be a cuckoo when, in fact,
I was a pair of binoculars looking at a cuckoo. I hung
around your neck, swaying on the drive home, where
you left me on the seat. There, I turned into a mote
of dust. The next day you sat in silence – the churring
call of a nightjar outside – while I nested in your eye.

3

Once I was a cucumber and you pretended I was
useful, but when I said I was a *Gurke* – speaking
German fluently – you tried to pickle me.
I remember wanting to turn into a kitten or
something cute but ended up as a novelty
keychain for a real estate broker called *Big Dick's*.

4

Once I was the chlorine in a public swimming
pool and I flowed into the open gills of a woman
I believed to be my mother, before it occurred
to me that my mother isn't young and doesn't have
gills. I turned into a macrophage and was able
to see that the woman I believed to be my mother
was addled with cancer, so I started to eat my way
through every cell I came across. Not because
I wanted to save her, but because it tasted good.

5

Once Europe was a market square and though
it wasn't market day I had come to sit and drink
hot chocolate and listen to the buskers, one of
whom was singing Schumann's *Dichterliebe*, which
for some reason you thought was *Bleeding Love*.
It's not, I said, but later I heard Leona Lewis's
voice in the flapping of the pigeons outside
the National Museum. The exhibits, on loan,
had been replaced by photographs. Each time
I tried to touch one, it moved. *You better back
the fuck off*, said the security guard. I turned
into a boy and girl who had lost their parents
and we hugged each other, crying.

6

Once the rain fell in vertical girders and I thought
I could walk between them, pressing my cheek
against their cold surface, but a mansion rose
about me several floors high and a voice called
telling me to leave. *Father*, I said, *why have you
forsaken me?* I turned into a great eyeball and
still he looked away, so I turned into a frog
and slipped without a sound into a millpond.

7

Once I was not myself or another man or either of
their lips exactly but the expression of a kiss they shared
and, at first, I have to say it was beautiful, but then
I felt myself turning into – or, no, recognizing
myself as – a desert flower, which was even better.

Yellow

The 'marvellous Chinese conjurer' Chung Ling Soo, born William Ellsworth Robinson, died on 24 March 1918 attempting to catch a bullet on stage. He had modelled his appearance and act on the contemporary Chinese magician Ching Ling Foo, born Zhu Liankui (朱連魁), who died in 1922.

Think of Chung Ling Soo who,
a century ago, his smooth
face greased and pigtail
bobbing, brought the wonders
of the East to the London
Hippodrome. A blend
of grace and speed, his face
impassive as a clay
soldier's, he was an early
master of the linking rings
and wove a braid so fine
they say he made of it
a gift to the Empress
Dowager.

      Now think of
Ching Ling Foo, a conjurer
from Peking who one day
browsing through the news
caught sight of Soo's
impassive face (his own
but strange) and went to
London – midwinter, mid-
Depression, fog so thick
the rooftops looked like they
were under sea – to call

his double out. Drunk suitors
followed day and night,
pulling at his hair. He did
two shows. No one came.
He grew impatient, wrote in
bluntly to *The Times*, then
turned a row of empty
seats into a flock of geese
and disappeared.

            Now think of
Soo and Foo at the same time
but separately: a blue sky
as reflected in a clear blue lake,
water above and water
below. There's Soo doubled-
over on stage, gun smoke
clearing, real blood running
down his long silk shirt,
shouting *Lower the curtain!*
A nasal brogue (his own
but strange) rings through
the theatre, fades.

            Somewhere
in a corner of the Yellow
River Valley, Foo is sleeping
underneath a pinkish plum tree,
dreaming he's suspended
by his ankles in a sealed
water tank, pigtail floating

up across his eyes. He tries
to pull the loose knot free
but only pulls it tighter.
Bound and gagged he feels
the muscles slacken
from the back of his neck
down to his anus, his
calves, his anonymous
toes, around which billows
the yellow squit of his
final movement.

Pathetic Earthlings

Planet Mongo is underdeveloped in certain respects – most of its terrain
is purple rock – but they do have hovercrafts and telepathy so while
you're flying from the imperial palace to visit your cousin beyond
the purple rocks and the ice mound they call Frigia you can put
a plastic halo over your head and *think to* your cousin, as the Mongo
people say, and be talking to him as if you were inside each other's
head or on handsfree. Though impressive technologically, this has
one defect: you can't refuse to take a telepathic call. Suddenly
you're inside their head and they're inside of yours, and what if
your cousin is in a bad mood or having sex with his wife – or another
woman – or masturbating over something terrible. I have a cousin
called Ming and people say I look like him, which is uncomfortable
because, though he may not be evil, he's done bad things. When I
tell people this and say his name is Ming, they laugh because
(I assume) it's such an evil-sounding name. Ming doesn't wear red
suits trimmed with gold, isn't bald, and doesn't have facial hair like
a court jester's parted legs, but sometimes that's how I think
of him too. And if even I can't help thinking of him like that then
maybe he couldn't help becoming kind of evil over time. I *think to* him,
my hovercraft skimming over the purple wastes of Planet Mongo,
and enter his consciousness just as he sits down on the toilet,
malaria-obsessed, the only decoration in his bathroom a picture of
his daughter he can't look at now without crying, wondering
when it was his life turned so thoroughly fucking evil. He didn't
start out wanting to be rich and powerful or to sleep with anyone
other than his wife necessarily. I could be *thinking to* him more mercy
than he would himself allow. We haven't spoken in nine years.
Perhaps, like Emperor Ming, he's only sitting in his version of a palace,
eyebrows arched, tormenting *pathetic earthlings*. I *think to* him,
I really do, but you can never know for certain whose head you're in.

Glass Case

My grandad introduced me to shallots, which he would fry in butter with chopped potatoes. I wrote about this once and a friend said I'd made a fetish of the word shallot – or was it a reference to *The Lady of Shalott*? When my grandad died I thought that only suffering was real and happiness pain's absence. I told myself that art should be like glass. When Hart Crane sings *the silken skilled transmemberment of song*, his pained voice carries across (or through) unmaimed. No one should have to say they're sad.

              Reverend Flint's gift of his uncle's
              Dutch East Indian artefacts
              to the British Museum means that
              two of Sir Stamford Raffles' wayang
              masks collected during his time as
              Governor of Java sit behind a glass case
              in the Enlightenment Gallery
              he lives on in them or through them
              for counterpoint they have been
              placed beside two mummified heads
              one of which retains the bandaging
              that has corroded from the other

When Mum first came to London, she waitressed at a Thai restaurant in Gants Hill. She says the prawn toast would always slip off the plate as she made to set it down and one day she spilt a whole plate on that guy who hosted *Restoration*. Over three decades later, Chinese Indonesians are still keeping their heads low – neither China nor Indonesia is home – and here, as ever, the self must be embodied or, like those oily sesame seeds on Griff Rhys Jones's pink shirt, embedded.

OTHER, MIXED is what I tick
in forms though some
drunk nights I theorize my own
transmembered norms

What have you taken?   What you have taken

What you have taken from me

I have taken nothing from you

What have I taken?

Then I have taken nothing

What you have taken

What have you taken?

40

Scene Change

A row of Georgian
houses slopes
down to a meadow

filled with pretty
little meadow
flowers where

you could forget
these rolling
barrows started

life as stacks of
corpses piled
high with earth

and stone that
rotted back into
the land and

only after several
generations'
growth grew

to resemble
what you might
call scenic

*

Built by the Dutch
in the century
before last

I climb the high
steps of the
bell tower and

taking in my
hands the tongue
the clapper

ring too slowly
at first aware
of my imposture

and then too
quickly in a bid
to compensate

as it dings hollow
across the
square and down

across the car-
polluted outskirts
of the colony

3/

Break

I go downstairs, unlock the door and take the coffee pot
outside where I empty the grounds beside the trunk of a tree
that must have died before you moved in but which
I'm hoping to revive with coffee. It might have been
a palm tree once, though now it looks like Gandalf's
withered staff. I spoon out the last wet grounds, runny
as the stool of a sick dog, and ask if I should feel
ashamed that instead of emptying the grounds after
finishing I wait until the next day. But it's fine, isn't it?
I mean, if you were here you might complain
but you're not – we're on a break – so it's probably

fine. I decide to set the poetry group a new assignment:
to write *into the break*. I look up references to breaks
in the Bible. The Book of Job has most. Job is broken
repeatedly: *He breaketh me with a tempest*; *He breaketh
me with breach upon breach, he runneth upon me like a giant*;
*How long will ye vex my soul and break me in pieces with
words?* Still, Job goes on trusting God. There is
a Sharon Olds poem about sex in winter where she
describes her lover as *like God*, but rather than vex her
he runs his palm over her face and sends her down
to be born. The left-hand margin is like the trunk of a

tree, each line break seeming to lead us, fronds shaking, out
into the air. Who is this us, though? For both our sakes
we haven't spoken in over a month, but still I frame
my thoughts as if they were to you. I empty the coffee as if
you were here, not in the sense that I talk aloud to you
or picture you standing there, but in that I'm aware of
something in me broken. That doesn't mean unhappy.
I put on music and all I hear are breaks: the drum break
in 'When the Levee Breaks', as sampled by Dr. Dre in
'Lyrical Gangbang'. The solo break in 'Chasin' the Trane'
that John Coltrane was shown transcribed and couldn't

understand. The band drops back – is broken free of –
and he moves beyond the song's constraints, but only so as
to make space for what follows. Heartbreak. Breakdown.
Breakthrough. Beneath the surface flow of time are nodes.
You slip into the break and look around, see past and future,
love and sickness rearranged. *Reordered*. You feel yourself
both whole and breached. As me you. As you do. After
the break, the band joins in. Everything and nothing is
the same. Everything and nothing is after. I wonder if before
dogs lose consciousness they know themselves as dying or
if it's as I imagine, like daylight breaking through an open door.

Buddleia Not Buddha

chanting in bloom my soul before
I knowed it chanting too
I ran down to the tube and from
Gray's Inn Rd to Farringdon
to the Golden Lane Estate
    buddleia not buddha chanting in bloom
I went not caring where I
went how late it was or why but
barred at every turn I took
and every church gate chained
    buddleia not buddha chanting in bloom
grey it grew and far from home
until I had to stop – my bundling
found me on a bus and eyes closed
there I cried waiting for the sky
to gape and let me crawl inside
    buddleia not buddha chanting in bloom
    buddleia not buddha buddling on my tomb

From the other side of Shooter's Hill,

you saw an ambulance speed past
a row of stationary cars, though at a distance you couldn't hear
the siren and it looked to be moving slowly like a police car in a silent film
(driving slowly so as to appear at a normal speed in playback)
and you thought you saw the Keystone Cops crowded into a single car
chugging along the road to your little niece's birthday party
where they would fall over themselves in a heap at her doorstep
and you started crying. And when you arrived at my flat you told me
about the ambulance and the Keystone Cops and started crying
again – I did too – and I asked if everything was OK. Yes,
everything's OK, you said, suddenly embarrassed, but wait,
why am I telling you this? Don't you dare think about using me
in a poem, making me into some sad female cypher, my life
a series of symbolic events: the ambulance representing mortality,
my niece – I don't know – a hysterical desire for kids. Hey hey,
I said, what about the Keystone Cops, how do they fit in?
If I say this in a poem, it isn't to defer responsibility but because
I reject the possibility of narrating any life other than my own
and need a voice capacious enough to be both me and not-me,
while always clearly being me. Fine, you said, pouring us
a cup of black tea. Once, I said, changing tack, I was given
a pellet gun for my birthday and without my knowing a friend
started aiming it at passers-by – or, he claimed, at pigeons –
until a neighbour called the police. In his defence he asked how
anyone could mistake the puck of a pellet gun for that of a real gun.
He sounds like a real jerk, you said. Starting to relax, to laugh,
you told me about a recent dream in which you were trapped
in a silent film, your every movement seen as slapstick, no one
able to hear you scream. Maybe we should watch some Percy Stow,
I said, and put on *How to Stop a Motor Car*, a minute-long silent film
featuring a car that slices a policeman in two before bouncing off

another man's butt. Hilarious, right? But it's Stow's 1908
version of *The Tempest* that's his masterpiece. He has Ariel,
freed from the bole of an oak tree, do a curtsey – she's just
a child – and scare off Caliban by turning into a monkey.
How great is that? But the cast, you said, who are they? A bunch
of Edwardian amateur actors and enthusiasts. The girl
who plays Ariel might even have been the daughter of one.
She must be dead, you said. Obviously, I replied. But by this stage
in the evening I was tired, my lips moving slowly, and though
I could see you were in distress it was like the ambulance you saw
moving slowly, silently across the other side of Shooter's Hill.
I do want children, you said, but not yet, not in this world.
In playback, I knew, not only would we appear to be talking
comically fast, but it would be impossible to tell who was speaking.

The Hanged Man

He bought a seeded loaf and two ripe and ready avocados
and left them in the hallway, and at lunch the next day went
to Chipotle on Charing Cross Road, then back to work,

and afterwards bought a ring doughnut from Tesco
because there were no jam doughnuts.

That night, though he didn't think he was a hoarder,
he started ordering records online and soon he had bought
the whole of Bruce Springsteen's back catalogue.

I hate Bruce Springsteen, he thought. *I want to eat better.*

The next week, listening to *Human Touch*, he dozed
and woke to find himself floating two feet off the ground.

Hanging there. His parents were alive and dead.
If only he could keep completely still he could remain
unscattered, forever on the edge of rain.

Another Life

There was the pasture of the green-room carpet
and the corridor which took you by the sound room
to the bar and artists' lounge, where a plate
of cold samosas had been left by the coffee machine.
I found the dressing room empty and sat there
staring at the mirror, at the big light bulbs
and concrete walls. *Bamboo*, I said. Its sound
dropped from my mouth without a sound. The TV
showed the next round of poets on stage.
A short white man described his burning hayrick
in a dream. An angel's crumpled wings. A tent?
I heard in him a vision of Old England
untouched by foreign hands. *Bamboo*, I said,
and leant my head against the wall the way I do
on buses. Two weeks ago, a couple laughed
at a woman walking by who had a Diet Coke
in one hand and the other held above her head,
her hood down, dancing. The wind blew
and she nearly lost her balance but not only did she
not fall, she performed a kind of hop
and skip. The poet spoke about the fall.
Nature fallen, his fallen nature. Still sat in
the dressing room, I travelled back in my mind
along the corridor and taking a different turn
pushed wide the fire exit's double doors
and walked into his dream. There was the hayrick,
removed from any idyll, piled high by
the bus stop, burning with a molten furore.
Beside it was a tent, half-collapsed, where
sleeping bodies lay. I heard the sweet collusion
of the crowds in bars and restaurants by the river.

The stairway leading to the Hayward Gallery
framed a strip of sky, the moon and stars
not stitched into its fabric yet. I thought of
Leicester Square in 1980 when my mum,
at the end of her secretarial course, about
to fly home, met my *bule* dad on the dance floor.
His purple flares. Her over-sized glasses.
She pretends to be embarrassed. *Discos aren't*
romantic! But just the thought of stepping out into
another life like that. I stood by the hayrick
and pictured him thatching it carefully, knowing
he would set the thing he loved ablaze and burn
inside of it. The wind blew. I did a Morris-style
hop and skip. It was autumn and the river's tent was
breaking. Rustle of leaf and russet falling. Mum
was dancing with the white man she would marry,
pleasure shaking through her leaves. And shame.
At least in her case it was real. The country
she would leave behind was real. *Bamboo*, I said.
Enlarge the place of thy tent. Set its stakes
so wide as to leave no one unhoused. Within
the dressing room's four sound-proofed walls,
the words dropped from my mouth without a sound.

All the Birds Are Your Husband

A tree felled four years ago.
   I feel it still. But not with
guilt. Reverberating in
   me. My rickety city.
My freight train. My empty din.

   Decades back. On Baker Street.
A van cut past. Skidded we
   did and fell fast. Socks wet. Blood
and fluff. What did I find. My
   eyes fixed on that van man's scared
face. Then Dad's. The frayedness there.

   Eggs and chips. Chips dipped in eggs.
Dripping yokes. Runny. Honey
   coloured. No jokes today please.

See me slumped against the door.
   Up to my knees. Shouting not
to be shut out. Outside the
   weeds grow four feet tall. Prideful.
Green. Mocking us baroquely.

As Chinatown in Jackson
    Heights is really town-sized. More
China-like than China. Whose
    steamed buns assume. Whose waving
kitties assume. Nothing. Not
    of me. So with Liverpool's

Chinese lanterns. Tree-tangled
    knots of them dangling freely
outside H&M. They make
    me think of you. They are not
light but light hosted. Shaking.

    She. Maybe he. Already
four years dead. No heraldry
    to brag of. And no body.

There must be some hard limit
    to language. To stop a thing
from living is to kill a
    thing. This sound stopped in my throat
is not a word. But could be.

One day I heard a woman
    started writing poems to
a friend with cancer. Not to
    comfort but to mock him. And
when he died she wrote poems
    to his wife. Mocked her too. She
told her that the birds in her
    garden were him. Her husband.
So she would sit outside and
    feed them stale crumbs. Until they

flapped away. And then she raged.
    Strange things started happening.
Her lights blew. Strings snapped on an
    unused harp. She shouted at
the new birds. One of them flew
    straight into her room. Shitting.
Screaming. What of the poet.

    She scolded the wife in her
most mocking poem yet. No.
    All the birds are your husband.

My head lay flat against your
        stomach. Love. *I made me down
a pallet on your floor.* Hurt
        was soft and low. The landing
where that wonky wardrobe door

        hung open. Day and night. In
sleet or snow. Dank landing. High
        blue sky outside. Shouting not
to be shut out. Screaming and
        crying. Crying and screaming.

In here is her. Her inheres
        to here. To its clear statement
of fact. I see her beckoned
        near. And nearer. Here. In us.

It hurts to look at what can't be
    because it wasn't. To look
therefore at what must be. What
    is. My sunstruck eyes. I twist
away. But a black echo
    rings round everything I see.

At the clinic. Browsing through
    a piece about punishment.
Punishment is payback. Is
    taking back what's owed with pain.
Still I moan. I whine. Still. That
    frayed face by the roadside mine.

When the wide sky wakes crying
    I feed it milk. And weakened.
Lulled. It's soon asleep. Sleep tight
    I say. My milkwhite darling.

Death can't take what can't be. And
    this I wish for you only.

4/

SAY

A brick-sized block of grey stone washed ashore on which was carved the word SAY. My dad picked it up at low tide and two months later found another, and another saying LES. We worked out that rather than a command – like Rilke's *flow* – it was the name of an old firm, SAYLES, which sold refined sugar, with plantations in the Caribbean and a factory in Chiswick. As capital flows, accumulates and breaks its bounds, so too had SAYLES broken into various subsidiaries. Slipped, dissolved and loosed. You find all kinds of things at low tide. One time, a black retriever came wagging up to me with a jawbone in its mouth. What can't be disposed of otherwise   what can't be broken down – is taken by the river,

spat out or lodged in mud. The SAY brick took pride of place on our chest of drawers – masonry, defaced by time, made part of the furniture. My dad decided to give it to you, in part because you're an artist and he thought it looked like art, but also, which is maybe the same, because it suggested reason in madness, and made him – made us – less afraid. Last week, there was an acid attack. Two cousins, assumed to be Muslim, having torn off their clothes, lay naked on the kerb, calling for help. Passers-by crossed the road. Things break, not flow; it is impossible, however lovely, to see the whole of humanity as a single helix rotating forever in the midst of universal time. Flow, break, flow. That's how

things go. Is it? What are you trying to say? After the operation, they stapled shut his stomach. As the scars healed, it became harder to discuss. He drank as if he had no body – nothing said, admitted to or broken. Flow, break, flow. Gather up the fragments. Now he is back to saying *The country's full. Why are they all men?* Four months ago, in a flimsy hospital gown, the fight had almost left him. In a tone you'd use to distract a child, the nurse told my mum about her holiday to Sumatra in the early 90s. *He likes custard*, she replied. We told him when to cough and when to breathe. He clasped a button that controlled the morphine. Bleep. Bleep. What did the blue and green lines mean? The sudden dips?

What was the nurse's name? I chose not to keep notes. Thoughtful as moss or black coffee, or as the screen of a dead phone. That's what eyes look like when you really look at them. Inanimate. Moss, though, is alive enough to harvest carbon dioxide, to grow. Yesterday I googled *thoughtful as moss*, thinking it was from a Seamus Heaney poem, but only found a description of the poet *grown long-haired and thoughtful; a wood-kerne escaped from the massacre.* At school, we learnt that wood-kernes were armed peasants who fought against the British in Ireland. I imagined them (and him) as thoughtful kernels, seeds that had escaped death by being spat out. I am nothing so solid or durable.

What are you trying to say? For years I made patterns in the air, not knowing what to say, then you came and pointed out the paintwork cracked and bubbling on the wall beside my bed which, though it stank, I hadn't noticed. The streetlight sparked on beads of damp. Your skin smelt bready, warm. I couldn't say how bare my life had been. The stillness in the room was like the stillness in the air between the heaves of storm. We flowed into and out of each other, saying – *what?* Saying. Not yet together, we were incapable of breaking. Cradled in pure being. The paint flaked, exposing streaks of poxy wall. I remembered a church where the saints' faces had been scratched away, taking on a new

expression: alien, afraid. Some days I must look alien to him. Scary. One poet said the devil was neither *blate nor scaur*, incapable of being scared. I sleep scared most nights but feel no more holy. Once I pronounced 'oven' *often* like my mum does, and a friend laughed. The cracks appeared beneath me. In the years before we met, though I wrote,

I was too scared – too scarred – to speak. Flow, flow, flow. I wanted to be carried along, not spat out or upon. That s AY brick picked from the riverbed proved that broken things still flow. *What are you trying to say?* When you asked me that I closed my laptop, offended. Why? It never mattered what I said. Whether you speak up or scarcely whisper,

you speak with all you are. To the eye of a being of incomparably longer life – to God or the devil – the human race would appear as one continuous vibration, in the same way a sparkler twirled at night looks like a circle. In darker days I couldn't say that to my dad, slumped in front of the TV with a mug of instant coffee. Saying it now only makes me think of times I've held a sparkler – the hiss and flare, the after-smell – which runs counter to that whole vision. One morning, gagging on his breathing tube, he started to text my mum, but before he could press send his phone died. He couldn't remember what he tried to say. I can't remember what I tried to say. Flow, break, flow. You hear me, though?

Half Got Out

I was reading a poem
by Ben Jonson where a
newborn *half got out* sees
the city burning and
decides to crawl back
into his mother's womb
thine urn he calls it it
was Tuesday morning
I'd just seen Leo near
Leicester Square he
was reading a book by
W.S. Merwin a poet
himself newly returned
to his dead mother's
womb *I was feeling so
anxious* Leo said *kind of
low when I started to read
him it felt like I found
him at just the right time*
I'm not sure but don't
parents always talk about
their kids arriving at
just the right time like
you might describe
finding your flip-flops
just before a beach
holiday yes I said to Leo
he wrote that poem
didn't he the sad dad
one that starts

My friend says I was not a good son
you understand
I say yes I understand

he says I did not go
to see my parents very often you know
and I say yes I know

I love the way the
dialogue loops back in
on itself the way you
know the poet is really
talking to or about
themselves it hurts to
read it it reminds me
I could be seeing my
parents right now who
live ten stops away *yes*
half an hour but I'm
not and what else am I
not doing *you have to*
work though you have to
make a living don't you
that may be true I
don't know I left the
library in light rain to

meet Sophie for a drink
at The Chandos and she
told me her granddad
used to go to Richmond

Park to fish he was a
wireless operating
sergeant during the war
it's not like she cares
it's just funny you know
even if she had a Victoria
Cross taped to her
forehead it wouldn't stop
those dickheads at the
bar from asking if she's
Latina or something
I just fucking hate this city
you understand I say yes
I understand *but I don't*
know how to leave it I say
yes I know I mean sorry
I don't know I don't
know how to leave or
where I'd even go

I looped back to enter
the tube at Leicester
Square stepping over
the body of a homeless
man to travel further
again from my mother's
womb to Turnpike Lane
the word *interred* echoing
in my head how many
acres of earth were there
above me then the

whole city might have
been burning I could
already have been dead

there's no going back my dad
said but how many times
have I crossed the point
of no return only to
crawl back down King
St or Goldhawk Rd
to eat chicken noodle
soup and talk about seat
cushions from Lidl *yes*
I know they're good value
thank you for dinner thank
you half got out and
half enwombed I know
that's just the way it is I
understand the tube
threading me like a
complex stitch beneath
and through the city
back to the house we've
been sharing lately
when I got in I said I'm
home and you said *yes*
I know and then you
filled the kettle and sat
down next to me and
said

RENDANG

1

Yathu tells me that last night he was in Stamford Hill and let himself be led into a stranger's kitchen. An old man wanted him to turn on his heating. He found the switch set above the counter by a bowl of fruit, almost hidden. And though it was past midnight he could hear the sounds of children playing in the hall.

(How scary it is, that moment before sleep takes hold. I used to put a circle of soft toys around my head to see me through, my echidna's small beak pointed like a spear. And even then when I heard the rustle of waterproof trousers, footsteps outside, a bag being packed and readied, I was scared. *It's me. Just me.*)

I ask if the man seemed grateful.

No, says Yathu. *It was just like it was the most normal thing for him to do.*

2

One summer, aged twenty, I was in Chicago looking for the flat of someone called Hayley, who had offered me a couch for the night. Lost on W Division St I saw a service station painted with a mural: a Puerto Rican couple, arm in arm, staring up at the two-pronged tip of the Sears Tower.

Bicycles circled the cantina
opposite, kids screaming
at each other from behind
their handlebars, looking like
they passed between
themselves a cup – not
like a trophy, more a kind
of chalice – because they
seemed to be going through
the motions of waiting and
wanting to put to their lips
the brim of a cup or trying to
grab at one, and none
of them, not one, noticed
the Sears Tower which
I now realized was directly
in front of us, the real
thing, its hulking bull-horns
framed by two high tenements.
Their shoulders turned
and hunched, laughing,
they pressed to their lips
the brim of an invisible cup.

Hayley's place was virtually empty:
a pile of clothes, a postcard of H.D., a framed
copy of *The Velvet Underground & Nico*.

I curled up on the floor and slept.

                              SLAM.

Flash of red and blue.

                    Hey there – hello!

                              HELLO!

Have you seen what's going on?

Outside!

Hayley was standing by the door. She peeked
through the blinds. Clicked them shut. Then
slid her hand behind the fridge. A striplight
flickered on.

I craned my neck above
the sill. Enough to see – or think I could –
an oily substance. Drops leading from
the kerbside to a body. White
sneakers.

Hayley wanted to cook so
made us scrambled eggs with onion and
cumin seeds. *Tex-Mex*, she said. Served
on the underside of a pink frisbee.
No plates. We listened to music, sirens
screeching behind us. Her new favourite
thing was dubstep.

Wait. Didn't you say
you were from London or something?

3

As soon as Yathu said *bowl of fruit* I pictured the banana on the front cover of *The Velvet Underground* LP. The striplight flickered. Yathu and Hayley fused. There was the openness with which he walked into that old man's home, the same way Hayley opened hers to me. A stranger. And there was another, more important aspect to his openness (like Hayley's, unexpectant): the lack – or need – of gratitude.

4

Yathu talks about his mum
and I talk about mine, neither
of whom were born in this
country. I mention the bedsit
in Cricklewood where my parents
lived, how my mum squeezed
all her belongings into its one
wardrobe, stuffing the rest
under the bed, adopting
my dad's strict diet of spam
and eggs.

       Younger than I am now,
she put an electric kettle on
the hob and nearly set the house
ablaze.   *Fire fire fire!*
Her whole life like that plastic
handle burnt out of shape.

Yathu's mum describes her life
in Sri Lanka as a thread
on which various events
were strung that she could
recall at will. But when
she came to London the cord
snapped. Her life became
a single point, all of its moments
converging on one spot.
Again and again.

5

Early mornings some nights,
my circle of soft toys close
around my head, I'd hear my dad
carry his bags to the scooter.
I wanted morning but I feared
to sleep.

The contractions
went on for so long Mum says
he left the hospital to look in at
an antiques fair but was back
in time to hold her, to hold
her hand as she shook
and swore, praying it would
stop.

Some mornings I wake up
early enough that it's still
dark and I can imagine myself
unborn. I lay the pages
of this book around me.

I talk to them. *RENDANG*,
I whisper. *RENDANG*.
No, they respond. *No, no.*

6

Hayley wanted to take us to a mezcal bar called Papa Ray's. As she closed the gate, paramedics were lifting a man onto a stretcher. A cordon had been set up. A blond man, wearing headphones, walked past.

HAYLEY: Hey, Brooks!

BROOKS: [*turning around*] Hayley! Long time no see.

HAYLEY: I thought you'd headed to Humboldt . . .

BROOKS: That's next semester. Things are pretty crazy. You know what's been happening here?

HAYLEY: [*explains quietly*] . . . but what about you?

BROOKS: Not much, what with schoolwork and Labor Day coming up.

HAYLEY: Hey, you want to come to Papa Ray's with us?

Just then the man
I thought I was
looking at looked
up at me and he
wasn't a man
as such but a boy
one of the boys
I'd seen joking and
shouting outside
the cantina one of his
eyes now swollen
shut I looked at him
and he looked up
at me and mouthed
Fuck off

or that's what I say he said

I must have been
too far away to see
but it feels true so
when I tell this story
I add that *Fuck off*

I don't know what I saw

a stretcher borne
calmly onto
an ambulance
the white sill
behind which
my head dipped
the dark leaves
of American elms
along a street
quiet as it is
outside the pub
where Yathu and I
are talking about
ourselves here now

7

Yathu says he went by Church St to find a gift for Mother's Day. He went into five shops and couldn't find a single non-white person, or anything his mum would like. *It was all so dainty.*

I tell him that recently strangers have been coming up to me on the street. Yesterday, for example, a man in Shepherd's Bush asked me about the fire.

> ME: The fire?
> HIM: Yes. Is it near . . . ?
> ME: [*silence*] Grenfell?
> HIM: Yes!
> ME: I don't know. Fifteen minutes?

I described the route and as I did
he smiled. Not in an evil way.
The opposite. Like someone on
a pilgrimage. And I watched him
walk down Goldhawk Rd, bagless
and alone, carried aloft by what
I assumed was some faith in
suffering observed as healing.
I thought about how I used to
hate going to Jakarta, being
implicated in the spectacle of
hurt. I couldn't bear to look at
it – to talk or think about it –
so I covered it in silence.
I cordoned it off.

Tonight I think
of nothing empty
and life not
sound or fury
hit out to a
random beat but
silence mainly
silence that
accrues weight that
takes up space
and yet contains it

8

In this memory's invented 'I'
I'm a child sitting in the corner
of my dad's old stall (now a GAIL's)
in Portobello. An open unlit
room. Dawn outside, overcast.
Don't worry, she says. *He's getting tea.*
A dozen antiques dealers
crowd around a tray of green
ceramic ducks. They hold them
close enough to check for
imperfections. Cracks. They look
with such care these might be
the new forms their past selves
took on overnight, their attention
an act of kindness to the past.

9

I wake up early enough that it's still dark and I can imagine myself unborn. Yathu and Hayley are talking somewhere, breaking apart the silence in me. In Stamford Hill and Shepherd's Bush, those strangers' faces beckon mutely. I hear the sounds of children playing in the hall. The far-off screech of fruit flies. See my circle of soft toys. That bowl of fruit and postcard of H.D. Striplight and stretcher. Tin of spam. I walk half-waking through my wakeless days.

RENDANG, I whisper.
RENDANG. I lay
the pages of this book
around me. I talk to them.

No, they respond. *No, no.*

NOTES

'Holy Man' quotes from John Clare's 'Meet Me in the Green Glen'. In 'State-Building', the Derek Walcott quotation is taken from his lecture 'The Antilles: Fragments of Epic Memory' (1992), as published on the Nobel Prize website. The 'thickest stars' in 'The White Jumper' are from Emily Brontë's 'The Prisoner'. In the same poem, Bob's dream is quoted from Alice Miller's *The Drama of Being a Child* (Virago, 1995). The loose version of Théophile Gautier is from 'Symphonie en blanc majeur'. 'Glass Case' quotes from the Hart Crane poem 'Voyages', published in *The Complete Poems of Hart Crane* (Liveright, 2001). In 'Break', the 'nodes' are inspired by Ralph Ellison's *Invisible Man* (London: Penguin, 2001) as riffed on by Fred Moten in *In the Break* (University of Minnesota Press, 2003). 'All the Birds Are Your Husband' quotes from the blues standard 'Make Me a Pallet on Your Floor', popularized by Mississippi John Hurt. 'SAY' quotes from 'Singing School' by Seamus Heaney, published in *Opened Ground: Poems 1966–1996* (Faber & Faber, 1998), and 'I heard a fly buzz' (591) by Emily Dickinson from *The Poems of Emily Dickinson* (Belknap Press, 2005). The line about speaking 'with all you are' paraphrases a section from Maurice Merleau-Ponty's *The Visible and the Invisible* (Northwestern University Press, 1968). The 'being of incomparably longer life' is from Arthur Schopenhauer's *The World as Will and Representation Vol. 3*, as published on gutenberg.org. 'Half Got Out' quotes from W.S. Merwin's 'Yesterday', published in *Migration: New and Selected Poems* (Copper Canyon Press, 2005).

ACKNOWLEDGEMENTS

Several of the poems in this book appeared in different forms in the following places: *Ambit*, *Granta*, the *London Review of Books*, *Spells: 21st-Century Occult Poetry* (Ignota, 2019), *Ten: Poets of the New Generation* (Bloodaxe, 2017), *The Literateur*, *The Poetry Review*, *The Rialto*, and *The Scores*. My gratitude to the editors of those journals and anthologies. Thanks as well to *Poets & Players* who commissioned 'Half Got Out' for a performance at the Whitworth in Manchester. 'Half Got Out' is also published in *The People's House* (ed. Helen Charman and Grace Linden). Thank you to Anna Sulan Masing who commissioned a piece about rendang for *Voices at the Table*. The initial concrete poem ('REND, RENDER') is taken from that piece and it provided the impetus for 'In West Sumatra'. A fellowship from the Arts Foundation in 2019 aided in this book's completion.

A number of poems appear in altered form in *All This Is Implied* (HappenStance, 2017). I'll always be grateful to Helena Nelson, my first editor, for having faith in my work when I didn't. Thank you to Rachael Allen, without whom this book wouldn't exist, and to everyone at Granta for their support – especially to Eleanor Chandler for her owl-eyed suggestions.

This book arose out of innumerable conversations and encounters. There are some people named in the poems (some names have been changed), but many others float lovingly in the background. I hope they know who they are and what they mean to me. Thank you to Helen Charman, Hugh Foley, Patrick Mackie and Joe Minden for feedback on these poems at various stages. Thank you to Niki Chang for your conversations and tireless championing. The support of Nathalie Teitler and The Complete Works family, along with Sarah Howe and Sandeep Parmar, has been invaluable. My love to Aisha, and to Mum and Dad.

These poems are spoken in memory of those who can't hear them: Tjandra Sari, aka Mak (1931–2018), Swadaya Sitiabudi (1923–1979), John P. Harris (1923–2003), and Emy van der Spek (1929–2002).